Dot's Pad

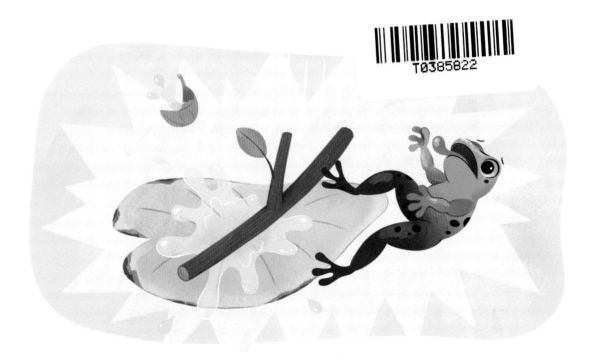

Written by Tanya Luther

Illustrated by Kristen Humphrey

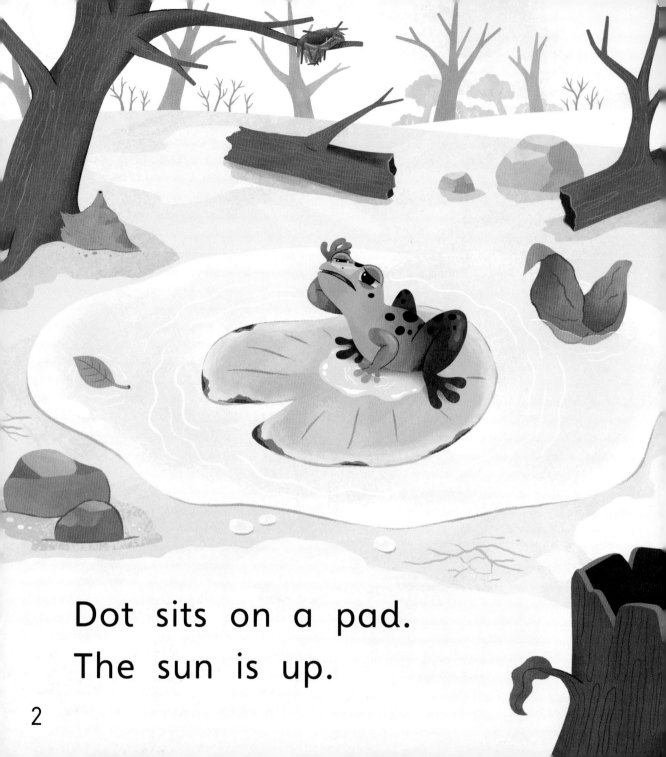

Dot sits on a pad.
The sun is up.

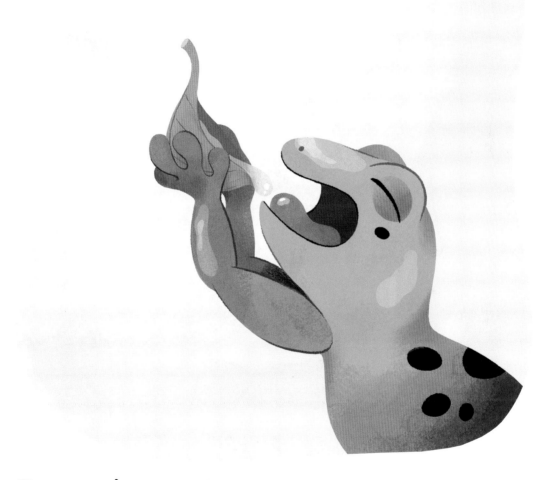

Dot sips at a cup.

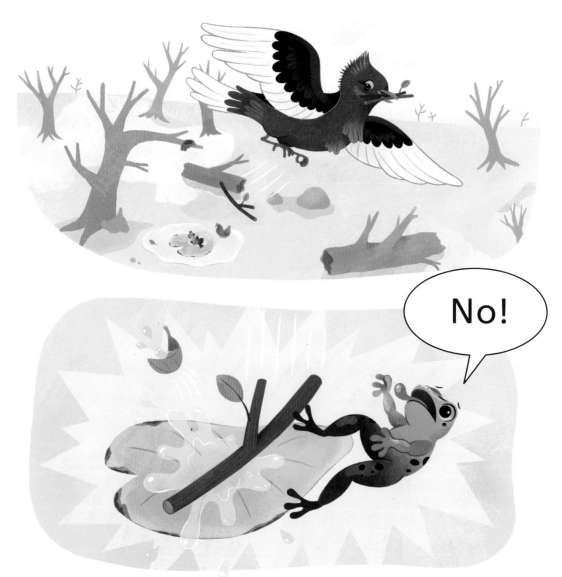

Red tips the pad.

Dot packs up.
The pad is a sack.

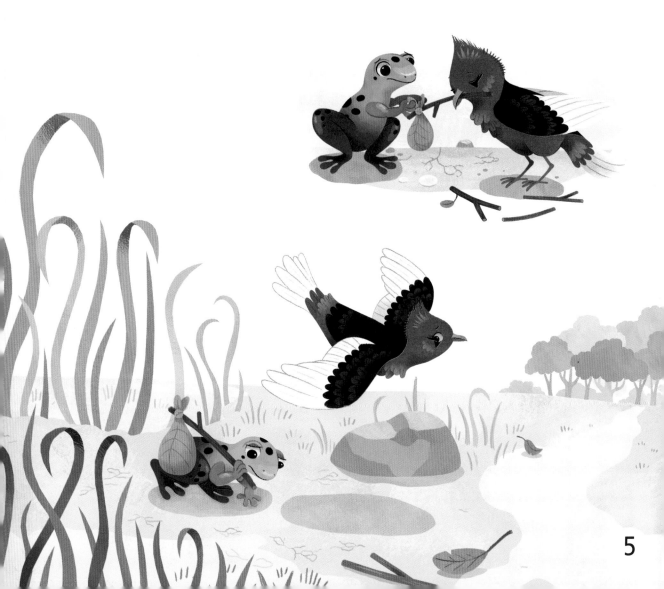

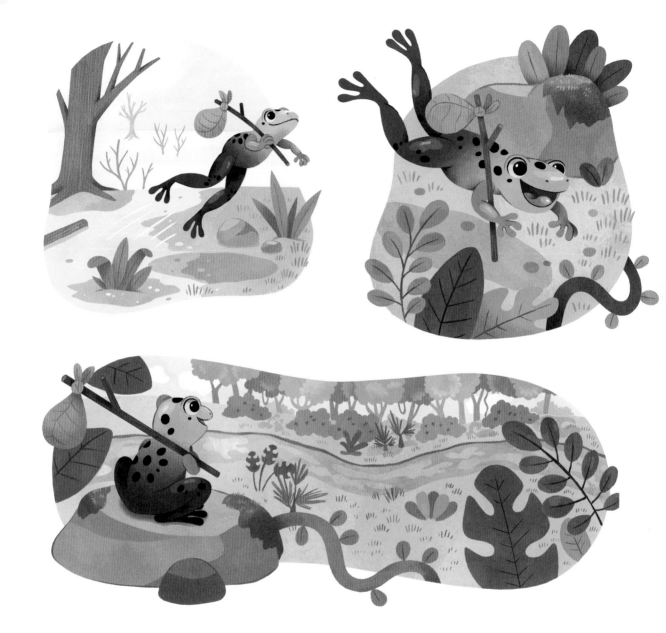

Dot gets to a rock.

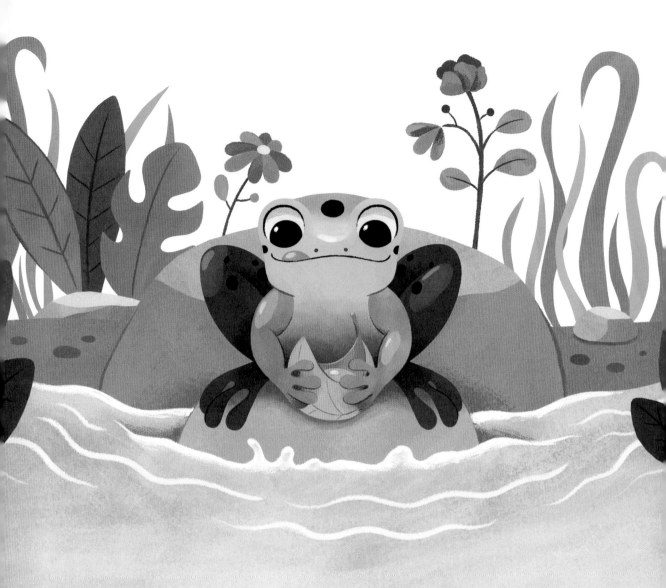

Dot dips the pad and sips.

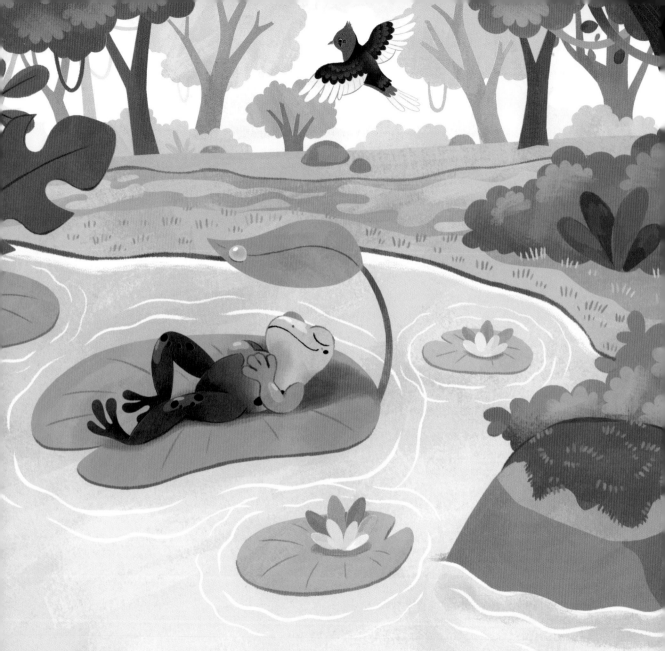

Dot naps on the pad.